FLOWERING AFTER FROST

THE ANTHOLOGY OF CONTEMPORARY
NEW ENGLAND POETRY

MICHAEL McMAHON, *Editor*

B|P
arti et veritatl

BOSTON
BRANDEN PRESS
PUBLISHERS

CREDITS

CONTENTS

FLOWERING AFTER FROST

ALLAN BLOCK

THE ANIMAL

(Deering, New Hampshire)

He floats a burnt auburn blur
over stone walls, through alder,
across the brittle surface of November.

If we could dismiss him as a young deer,
coyote, bobcat, wolf or fisher,
it might be easier to sleep up here;

but harried animals that we are,
we snag him in the mind, prefer
to cage and curry him, name him Fear.

CHILD'S DRAWING

A road is a crayon line. One bus
humps along it like a caterpillar.
A mountain sharp as an icepick
props up the sun, which ignites
three strenuous sunflowers.
A fish swims uphill. Those
V's trailing after him are not
birds, but his fins, an afterthought.
A small stick figure,
triangle for dress,
is signed in fervent yellow: JENNIFER
Green grass grows
where the paper was too white.

11

THROUGH OLD FARMHOUSE WINDOWS

Move your head and the view undulates.
Each pane is a watery lens. The apple trees

have rubber trunks. The road meanders more
than a road should. Even the modern house

on the next hill breathes a kind of passion.
From the attic's single, dollhouse window

we overlook a mirage of hay. Framed there,
the cattle stand, wrinkled as though by heat;

their spots wax and wane like shadow-play.
Our host, the farmer, sits teetering on his tractor.

Old glass can't distort him. He could be
any shape in his baggy overalls. Supper time

he clatters to the table, still trailing
mud and weeds and the day's irregular light.

IN THE GLUE FACTORY

I grind the hoofs of broken animals.
In a deep tub I mix an inscrutable batter.
It is a smell I would like to forget.

Taking up gobs in my fist I sling them
in all directions. It is my job to make a
mess and make it matter.

I have created a super glue nobody can doubt.
Applied to the soles of feet
it will bind men to their paths forever

without deceiving them.
To those who follow in my art
I swear there is no formula.

JANUARY THAW

In crow's-foot patterns, like deltas
seen from the air, the freeze runs off.

Five flawless days, under an azure sky,
the townsfolk come out to look. They nod

knowingly at the first smell of mud.
Jacketless, we hop from bog to bog

listening to the gurgle underground.
Up on the trail, we find last week's

snowshoe tracks, waffle after waffle.
The sun has burned them in like brands.

Mad rivers cut new rights-of-way.
The pines shake out their plumage. Bent

birches snap erect. Five days of this euphoria
and a raw wind turns our collars up.

Logic and January take over. Their glaciers
cannot be reversed or salted down.

As far as we can see in the blizzard
the sun is inhuman, like any other star.

IN NOAH'S WAKE

The giraffes already had sea legs.
Busy smelling out the corners, the moles
Were steady travelers. Placid too
Were the hibernating adders. It was the people,
Eternally on edge, who unbalanced the ark.
Uncles, country cousins, distant kin,
All handpicked, good churchgoers, they
Had been shepherded aboard ship
By a craven old man, and for what?
The rain came down, there was nothing to do
But continue in public the mutiny
Each had always conducted privately.
And, as it happened, they never struck
The right climate for regeneration.
Down in the hold, the beasts did better,
Egged on by what they thought was home,
Nothing clogging their pleasure, least of all
What the others rankled most over:
Stale fodder, cramped quarters, sour weather

46 & RECALLING

Nightmares have told me
I thought Mother my bride.
Something unspeakable we did

begat my brother, a big sad infant
who never slept. Normally
Father would enter here, but I

blotted him out, my dreams said,
as if he were vapor. From that point on
I hid my tenderness in one

book or another. My most recent
nightmare finds me oedipal,
smiling and smarting still

over that baby and my crime,
the sudden, bittersweet passion
having flooded me again.

Mother still lives, alone and wise,
Brother builds hospitals. I am what I am.
Father deserved a better friend.

FOUR HOMAGES

To a Portuguese Man-o-War

>   Your blue bladder
>   rides like an iceberg.
>   Laughing, you stab your friends.

To an Urchin

>   Come closer with your spines.
>   They are keen
>   as the needlepoint of stars.

To a Coral

>   Brain of a brain,
>   from now on
>   you prop up the house.

To the Sea Floor

>   For walking here I'll need
>   the plod of gravity,
>   the leverage of snails.

TARZAN, OLD

He walks on rubber knees. Oh Lord!
Something tells him his
hairlessness is not for Africa.
He wants words now, interviews,
last rites, a successor,
somebody to turn him under the grass.

HIGH TENSION WIRES

It is a universal network
Written across the sky,
Cut in swaths through the woods,
Amplified in cages
Marked "High Voltage." Its agitation
Planted from pole to pole
Gives palsy to the land.

Listen! Pressed up against my skull
Can you feel it running
Like a second bloodstream?
It is more than the electricity
Passed between us.
It is louder than
The chattering of teeth.

We know that somewhere, by a river,
Stretches the center of it.
Praised be Niagra,
Maker of our common music,
Killer of absolute silence,
The joiner of all lines,
For drawing us as we are.

LYN LIFSHIN

CEREMONY

All day they
bring the face
breaking open

The man who was murdered
spills against us,
an assassin still at large
across the screen

We unpack suitcases
anyway, never
not listening.
Loss keeps getting undressed
before our eyes

And microphone cables
catch in the reporters'
flesh like a
web of sea growth

dragging them
past cameras toward a
darkness of their
own tho
they appear to be
listing figures and
arrangements
calmly

tho their faces seem
with us,
comforting our air

18

with words
for the body falling over
and over

As if those linked in this
glow of pain
could never be alone

SNAKE DANCE

i rub the one bullet
i've ever held against

my lips put on his
old confederate jacket

we eat hardtack covered
with gold vermillion

high on an iroquois
spell we make each

other tremble (i could
be doing that snake

dance knowing about
things that bite and

what happens later still
taking them into my mouth)

LEAVING THEM, LETTING THE FARM SWALLOW

drove away i
know i'll never go

back and wanted
to write it down

the webs old
crosses, marys

horses against the sun
painted on

enamel on the walls

she said i don't see any
hope for the
world we just take
in poison

kneeling with
4 german shepherds
at one door the
daughter

singing how sweet it is

her white arms
dissolving in the
night grass

THE ORIGIN OF HOT AND COLD
ACCORDING TO THE DELEWARES

A man and a woman
started fighting, it was
far north and cold
so she went into
the hotlands. But
he got lonely, rode
south and brought
the cold. Wherever
he went it was
winter. They did
this every year

MONET'S LES NYMPHEAS

the long curved
room the walls

starting to
shimmer breathe

a chinese girl
sitting on the stone
bench next to me

dazed smiling

the lilies moving
into both of us

21

WAITING, THE HALLWAYS UNDER HER SKIN THICK
WITH DREAMCHILDREN

Lace grows in her eyes like
fat weddings,
she is pretty, has been baking

biscuits of linen to stuff into his mouth
all her life,

waiting for him. The hallways
under her skin are thick with dreamchildren.

Who he is hardly matters, her rooms
stay for him,

her body crying to be taken
with rings and furniture, tight behind doors

in a wave of green breath and wild rhythm,
in a bed of
lost birds and feathers,

smiling, dying

ON THE NEW ROAD

red sumac presses
against the windshield
tires moan

Your wife dreams
you are guilty,

I button and unbutton
what I feel

THAW

Ice comes undone
Skin shining and
hair full of
March

girls spill out of
offices their
bones whispering strong
hands to marry

glazed orchards
and vines coming back
Green is under the
snow the girls'

arms seem to open
as if to lift them past
fluorescent air
toward whatever

mysteries
are hidden from them
Later nearly
blinded by water and

light they'll
move a 1 o'clock wave
their hair folding
back into

rooms of
machines and paper But
no desks can
hold such

23

dreaming blood,
drunk on the poems
sun makes
in their bodies

NAMES

lately i become
whatever you call
me the way some
indians do (i'd
been wanting to
trade or sell or
bury a lot of
what I am too)
For six days i
couldn't say yours
because it was
someone else's.
When you called me
love near the rag
shop on caroline
i tried to remember
the spell iroquois
put on names to
make them stay

DEVELOPING CURIOUS SURVIVAL PATTERNS
AGAINST WINTER SALTWINDS THE

pitch pine
often stops
growing upwards
branches gnarl
close to the
dunes The
dead stand
erect for
years even
withered cones
stud their
branches and
salt and sand
until the whole
tree is covered
then plum and
bayberry take
hold, the way
poems sometimes do

WESLEY MCNAIR

FITZ HUGH LANE GOES TO THE MASTHEAD

"The difference with Lane is that he is principally concerned with revealing
nature's spiritual content. . . .On one occasion Lane [whose legs were paralyzed]
was hoisted up by some contrivance to the masthead of a vessel lying in
Gloucester harbor in order that he might get some particular perspective that
he wished to have."

John Wilmerding, *Fitz Hugh Lane*

Somewhere in California miners rise
up from rocks

to massacre the Pomos.
Already you are higher

wearing the face
that never could undo

its worry:
it is you who pass

the neat roofs
of the companies, leaving

uncounted barrels of fish & all
the merchants plotting

sea-routes to the West.
You are going straight up

past the white solemn
spires of churches

& oh it is so beautiful to
leave your legs

26

& to forget the Indians
who fall deeper

& deeper,
crying out for height

until the ship's sails open
behind you like wings

& you can see
Gloucester harbor & everything

beyond it
never happened.

THE CHARACTERS OF FORGOTTEN DIRTY JOKES

The boy who was once me
could tell each
traveling salesman what to do
with the farmer's third daughter
and the man at the whorehouse why
he has fucked a corpse.
They cry out
for their punchlines.
The wife's secret lover
whose balls accidentally dropped
through the closet keyhole
wants to know
what will happen next.
The scientist's maid,
having ordered the petrified dick
out of its special jar
and up her cunt,
can't make it stop.

None of them, not even an entire squad
of Foreign Legion volunteers
ready to screw anything,
can end their stories.
Salesmen who've been aroused
for twenty years
just wait. Insane with grief,
the maid
goes right on
fucking forever.

MEMORY OF KUHRE

killed by a tractor, August, 1970

hot days
the farm does not
move
far off
a cowbell far off
his tractor sound
caught in trees
& free again

i am there unsurprised
by my skinny arms
raking
in a field
i think maybe it will rain

but the clouds

move slowly they
are in another country
at dusk

28

the cows move back
into the field
like clouds
they dream themselves
walking shaking
flies from their sleep

mornings
the woman who talks
to the hens
throwing seeds &

it is me
listening
deep into the
tractor's
ponderous heart
for a spark
pulling the flywheel

i think
(it starts
up in such a rage)
how can the old man
hanging crutches
on the gearshift
climbing slowly
up its side
not be shaken
down

but each day

Kuhre
just lurches
off
into the tractor's
noise &

oh
it is such
a great slow
place the cows moving back
the clouds far
as continents
his tractor
circling
all my afternoons
& i am perhaps
thinking
his eye is gone

at supper
the woman crazy
with questions
i am thinking it

still

Kuhre sits
silent
& one-eyed
as his old
barn
& he never answers
he never

riding
out past cows
dreaming him
riding or it could be Kuhre's
strange shut
face
going by me
while i rake

until i think
part of him knows
something
it is night
or down
in a dim
green silo corn raining
all around
i rise slowly
upward
toward the light

& the morning
rises

it will be a
hot day
far off
the tractor sound
continues & the clouds
just continue

& it is me
watching
the woman among
the white
shrieking
of the hens throwing seeds
talking to them all

FIRE IN ENFIELD

Most days
the barn stands
across the street
from the washette,
high empty
windows staring into space
of another century.

Today, the barn's
on fire. People
roused from
the sleeping tenament
stand shyly among
their valuables:
a vacuum

cleaner, somebody's golden
reclining chair,
blank tv's.
Hope it don't
burn is
in their eyes.
Everybody here watches

water
from two hoses
unravel into the fire
like string.
The flames
do not hurry.
They belong here,

what the fat
man, tattoo blossoming

on his arm
perhaps knows.
The great
old roof
is open;

flames
take the air
like sails.
Skinny kids
watch the barn
sink slowly
into the earth.

THINKING ABOUT CARNEVALE'S WIFE

The only sign
advertises TIRE ALE
at Carnevale's garage.
Carnevale himself
stands under his sign
when you drive in,
waiting for your window
to reach him,
watching your tires. "Hello,
Dad," is what Carnevale says,
his business way of
disguising a bad memory.
I picture Carnevale
calling each of his children
"Dad," there are so many,
the oldest off fondling
their first
used cars, the youngest nearby
playing with hubcabs.

And when the red
gas pump begins to groan
and spin its eye
and Carnevale sings
in his unusually fine
tenor voice about lost love,
I usually think about
Carnevale's wife.
I have never seen her.
The gaping hoods
of cars in the grass
outside her house
utter no clues about
who's inside. Sometimes I think
she listens behinds her blinds
to Carnevale singing
while he pumps gas — a large woman
with a combustible
heart. Or
that it is washday
and she — a small, tired
woman — empties
all the family pockets
of bolts and piston rings.
Or I think that she is thin
and purposeful
and waits
for vats of Carnevale
TIRE ALE
simmering on the stove.

LEAVING THE COUNTRY HOUSE TO THE LANDLORD, FIVE YEARS LATER

For D.M.

Outside, the landlord undertakes the landscape
While he waits. He is ignoble
In his t-shirt, jiggles
A little above the taut power
Of his mower.

But he gets things done.
When he puts his chain saw once
Into our shade tree, it twists and falls.
Its branches look up startled
From the ground.

Inside, I curse him for coming.
It is in the dining room.
Blank walls undo the voice of my anger;
You look up from naming boxes
and shrug.

Behind you on the wall a hook has left
A hole open like a mouth.
I half see it, the way, taking out
Boxes, I notice your writing thin as tendril
and misspelled.

His family drives in.
The car is in love with size,
Wanders into the front lawn by our truck
And stops: its chrome grille tips and grins.
There's the big wife

Who came at supper once when light was amber
On our table and our books lay
Behind glass in another room and the cats
Riffled their bright fur, telling us how
She'd fix the place.

The children watched her flat voice hang
In the air. It was as if they were dreaming
She was there, they were so awed.
Closing a door on upside-down dining chairs,
I, too, am dreaming.

And the dream goes on. It will not stop; I can't awaken.
We are still moving out of the old cape.
In the front yard another tree
Has foundered. It leans on one side like
An exhausted fish;

The family outside seems underwater,
Moving onto the floor of the new space.
Slowly, the boyfriend is bumping the strange, angry
Saw against a branch. Blue smoke blooms
And rises.

The daughter is pleased — her sane
Skin wavers in the light. The wife
Is too big: in a kinder dream
She might lift slowly upward
Carrying her clear

Modern window planned for the upstairs
Far beyond the upstairs. But here
She just remains too big
And does not budge from earth.
Meanwhile, the landlord

Judges in his baseball cap the calves
Of the boy, how well they know
A motor. He is at home
With enterprise and things that go,
And when he shouts

Commands that drift sleepy as bubbles,
Inaudible above the raging saw,
We both can hear him say:
"You are awake. And what you've dreamed
Are your five gentle years."

THE LITTLE LOUEY COMIC

The idea was that Little Louey
the quiet well-dressed
little man of Sunday comics
had a gigantic prick
and was looking for some action.
Just when everybody at the whorehouse
was dying with laughter
to hear a middle-aged dwarf
announce his needs
he unzipped his pants and let it stretch
out like a leg.
Whores with helium tits stood around
open-mouthed. As for us coming
to know the quick mysterious
hard-on in study hall it was a transformation
better than Superman
and more possible. All of us dreamed
of Little Louey struggling to the top
of a high stool
to drop it like a bomb
on yawning cunts.

37

It was the way the great beast of dick
took on all comers and left
behind a trail of broken
jaws. We never stopped shoving
the comic in girls' faces
until our teachers horrified
destroyed the thing
burned Louey cactus balls
and all

except a scalloped comic bubble
rising in my mind from the spreadeagled legs
of women in wet-dreams film-stars
the wives of friends
bearing the words "I wanted fucked."

DAVID KHERDIAN

WHEN THESE OLD BARNS LOST THEIR INHABITANTS AND THEN THEIR PAIN AND THEN ALL SEMBLANCE OF DETERMINED HUMAN CONSTRUCTION

1.

They began to sway to the
forms of nature, desiring
some final ruin; desiring
some final ruin and return

2.

Their bodies ache and sway
to the rhythms of the
beckoning hills

3.

They carry in their burnt
wood the descending rays
of the setting sun

4.

Their windows are as small
as eyes

5.

They wish again to be a
falling tree

TWO PENNIES FOUND ON THE GRAVEL
WALK TO WINDSOR MOUNTAIN SCHOOL

TAKE ONE:

They are next to each other:
one forward, one back,
like an Oriental couple
out on a walk.

If more people didn't stay home
I'd be rich.

TAKE TWO:

I think I'll rub them together
to see if they will clean or
bring luck, before writing this poem.

SQUIRRELS IN WIND PINE

Squirrels from treetops listen to
pine wind song. Such overtures of
the season come again and again,
and today, after cloud change and
light rain, the heavy tender wind
comes to pine grove for lute song,
and to comb back animal hair.

Yesterday, the squirrels played all
afternoon in the sun. Today they
are silent among old leaves and
branches, safe in their nests.

In quiet, they give their secrets
over to the earth, and take them back.

LAKE MICHIGAN

That shore, with its seagulls,
    March wind, and snow
    banks pushed against
    the hill
Lay reposed upon itself
    as if it had never been
    entered by artist,
    tradesman, craftsman
    or traveler.

MY MOTHER AND THE AMERICANS

My mother, who
sees life at that
peculiarly oblique angle
that is commonly referred to
as artistic insight,
is the visionary poet
of the family,
        but fortunately,
(for those disciples who
hope to succeed her),
she doesn't practice her arts
outside the home

and one day,
looking out the window into
memory and the future,
she announced:
        "These Americans raise
their children like chickens —
    Any which way."

41

BECKONED IN DREAM TO THE UNCONSCIOUS

We are three, clearly three,
on precipice of rock
over churning water
where, forbidding
but seductive,
black and white sea lions play.

One thinks it easy and
would enjoy a ride
but suit of fur must be affected
for the ride in sealskin on another's side.
It appears so easy to live above
yet below.
         We do not know
this is a warning dream.

They show us angry teeth
but do not bite. The
largest comes to topple us
from the other's side.
Hurled, we struggle for return as other selves
reach out;
         to wakefulness and dread.

KATO'S POEM

O I remember in Duncan's Mills
the water lilies
flourished on the pond
and croaking frogs sat
on their leaves
as in story books.

JOHN STEVENS WADE

THE CLOTHESLINE

In the back yard
I can see the cloth lungs
of my old shirt suck in
the scoured wind. There is something
out there I've never been able
to slip on and button
up to my chin.

When I
was ten I nearly got
it on. I had been keeping
in step with the rinsed step
of underwear. One light-
footed spin, and I would
have swung with the starched bones
along the line.

Since then
I have become suspicious
of weights and measurements.
I take my wooden walks,
and I feel pinned whenever
I watch the handkerchief
behavior of birds; whenever
I study the weather for signs
of a high wind.

THE SMELL OF WOOD

There's something to think about
when you lay your head in the grass,
and the smell of dry sticks,
boned in the turf, reminds you
of kindling and a sharp axe.
It's then your sense of smell
brings back the man who looks
like you, but is a taut
rendition—younger, with axe
poised and muscles hard
as stove wood. You stand back;
you watch. His legs break from
their oak stance like dry-
rot, and a bolt
of steel strikes dead a block
of beech. You smell blood
as the sap jewels up
from the cramped veins; and the smell
takes you back with your head
in the grass, and you're holding
a dry stick. An object for
attention. Something to smell.

DAISIES

When it is plucking time for my young son
and I am *Father William* and wiser than my words,
I won't tell the boy what I know about honeycombs.
We'll sit upstairs and talk sex;
talk of that mysterious thrill
that leaves each blood cell tall
as a sunflower. If he should mention
daisies, I'll say: "Well, there was once

44

an ancient theory about such things . . ."
then my voice will fade as if I had forgotten.
I won't tell him that saying love-
me and love-me-not is just one
way of pulling a daisy apart.
Let him learn this from some woman
who will want him to make confetti
out of every field in sight. I'll just tell him
that women are wiser than we are
when it comes to the mystery of loving,
but of daisies, their knowledge is slight.

DAYS LIKE THIS

Days like this, I want to
go out and take off my clothes and put on
a cassock of dry leaves and carry
a crotched stick and get
down on my knees and give
the last rites to all the wilted dahlias
in kind Mrs. Higginson's back yard.
Then I would take off the leaves and strut naked down Main
and deliver the Gettysburg Address
to all pigeons and squirrels in the park.
I would lean against the stone arse
of Grant's horse and shout obscenities
in the name of Eisenhower, Custer, and Clausewitz.
Then I would dance back up Main like a Nureyev,
roll in Mrs. Higginson's dahlia bed,
break the crotched stick, tear up the dry leaves,
put on my old clothes, climb Mr. Higginson's back fence,
enter my own house, and say to my wife:
"I'm home, dear, back from my walk."

GARY LAWLESS

MOVEMENT

tough.
precise.
you
move
like
a cougar.

place your
steps
carefully.
correctly.

there are
no
wrong
moves.

THE AINU MEN

whisker dripping bear grin
    wild stump honey
paw berries & trout
pad heavy thru wet morning grass
long fur hot in sunlight
    morning bear sweat
    rustling brush
(wild hairy Ainu men down the coastline)

46

THE CONFESSION

I met with the gnat,
giant, sweating, fierce
and learned its secret.
I saw the world
revealed in Wovoka's black hat,
a feather passed over.
I came to knowledge
at an incredibly old age
and the light was strong,
it passed through me.
I performed healings
and sang the old songs
and traced lives back
to the time of beginnings,
to seek an ally, a power.
I no longer see the road,
only the wilderness.
(I shake now mornings when I wake up.)

HUNTING FRAGMENT

six days on snowshoes
running from storm starved wolves
chasing still warm body meat when I fall.
hours of light spent walking
lifting snowshoes out of powder
eyes near blind from the glare, squinted.
winds carrying man-scent
movement keeps them cautious.

little sleep at night
gathering, cutting wood for
a fire,

47

animals prowling
the edge of darkness
cruel eyes in the night,
paw prints in morning snow.
other nights covered by a poncho
safe in branches of a tall tree,
eyes open wide for bobcat.

leather bindings iced,
beard frozen, face raw
keep moving.

RAIL SPLITTING

wedges
     slide
into cracks—
logs split, ripped.
hammer, maul, axe.
primitive tools and rhythms.
"There's more Zen in this log
than in all your zazen.
You just have to find the weak spots
and hit 'em.

hot work,
close to the wood.
The control of
placing your axe
exactly where you wanted it.

GEORGE M. YOUNG, JR.

THE LECTURER SEEKS A WIFE

He darkens the boxes of desired characteristics:

Good looking but not too plump.
The kind who waits at home with a smile.

Cards keep spewing from the computor's mouth:
The thousand names and addresses of his skeleton.

He places an advertisement in a literary review:

"Suave academic, East Coast, Sagitarius,
Desires nubile Virgo
Interested in skindiving."

The picture arrives signed "La Passionata":
His skeleton recumbent in bikini and sunglasses
A longstem rose between her teeth.

At the singles bar he winks at seven dancers in seven miniskirts
But even in an orange wig
The one who winks back looks terribly familiar.

He wakes up with a hangover in a Tijuana motel.

How did that bone ring get on his finger?
Who etched that gruesome tattoo on his belly?

A weird thin voice stops singing in the shower.
She steps from the bathroom.
She drops the towel.

Well. He shakes his head. It could be worse.

LECTURES ON THE BIOLOGY OF THE SHADOW

I.   Where Do Shadows Live?

     Some prefer the quiet of an empty closet.
     The gregarious prefer closets filled with skeletons.
     Others—the vast stretches of space between neutrinos.
     Still others prefer none of these—their home is nowhere.

     But all shadows wait patiently for light
     Being by their nature true believers.

II.   What Do Shadows Eat?

     Bulletholes, canyons, pauses between ideas,
     Spaces between parked jeeps, the centers of wedding
        rings,
     What remains in glasses after all the wine is drunk,
     The insides of bubbles, credibility gaps. . . .

     Shadows are an asset to any economy.

III. How Do Shadows Mate?

     Where two fall together a third is made.

     Do not look into the third shadow.

     It embarrasses those mating
     It teaches nothing
     It begs the question

     It is said the third shadow funnels you to death.

IV.   Can A Shadow Find Happiness?

     IF we accept the stoic's definition:
     "Happiness is space vacated by desire"
     IF the old saying is also a true one:
     "Once a shadow always a shadow"
     AND IF as the evidence leads one to deduce
     Shadows are always notorious stoics

     Then many shadows too find happiness.

LECTURE BEFORE A LECTURE ON PUSHKIN

To your left is the Gettysburg Address engraved on a medalion.
To your right, The Lord's Prayer on the head of a pin.

The dot in the middle is War and Peace
Moby Dick and the Waverly Novels
skillfully etched not on the head
but on the japping point of a sewing needle.

Observe the shadows between the iambs,
the bell that accompanies each new rhyme.
You will note the whole is in capital letters
with big spaces in between.

Behind the letters the words extend for thirty versts.

Between the stanzas lie the Russian steppes.

It is remarkable to find so much on the point of a needle.

But tomorrow we shall turn to Pushkin.

THREE LECTURES ON THE SKELETON

I. Skeleton in the Classroom

Let us consider the skeleton inside the body.

You will observe that the body around the skeleton is dying.
You will further observe that the skeleton is grinning.

Do not ask why.
Davy Crockett did not ask why.
The Mona Lisa does not ask why.
Nor does a skeleton ever ask why.

It is best understood as a matter of molecules.

One authority claims to have solved the problem with an
    equation.

He grins back.

II. Skeleton in the Office

We begin with a student crying in an office.
Her life has been split open. The lecturer's
best words only increase the bleeding.

I draw your attention to the lecturer after the student has left.
Note how the thin bones inside his fingers
close on pencils he wants to put on the table,
reach for paperclips he wants to leave in the drawer.

Now it is noon.
The lecturer stops between bites of his apple and listens:
The teeth inside him are still gnawing.

Now watch the clock hands move.

Yesterday the maple leaf outside was green.

In a lifetime a skeleton devours fifty times its own weight.

It happens in offices all over America.

III. Skeleton at the Beach

We see a beach.
Two boys are playing a loud game of frisbee in front of
two girls in loosened bikinis who pretend not to notice.

Behind the umbrella an old man strokes his wife's back.

Are there not lovers everywhere?

Hand in hand a skeleton and a man go walking toward the sea.

POLAR EXPEDITION

Mais ou sont les neiges d'antan?
—Villon

The snows of yesteryear?

Try the North Pole.

A new expedition.
Destination—the enigmatic heaps.

From North Cape the expedition reports
All the Medians are converging!

It is a strange, cold god who lures his pilgrims
beyond the last fire
beyond the last hut
beyond the last green
to kneel under Polaris
where all the medians are together.

But so far they have only reached North Cape.

How many ruined castles lie behind the cliff they stand on!

From North Cape
antlers on their backpacks for antennae
they must learn to fly or walk on water.

53

THE WOMB IS RUINS

This is my coliseum
Old bath of the gods
I hear water and dogs
Guarding all the gates
Gladiators doze
Side by side like oxen
Archimedes strokes his slabs of gold
His pure commandments
This is the cobweb
Of a universe the spiders
Could spin away
The white stone powder
Bees mistake for pollen
Will not bloom
Still there are flowers here
Come, name them

CROQUET IN CHILDHOOD

We knock red yellow blue
twilight in and out of wickets
bent spines of invisible animals
we need to enter. The rhododendrons
are out of bounds and all the stars
shine before our colors strike
the final post. Long after

we toss our mallets in the flowerbeds
my drunk uncle plays alone.
His lit Havana hovers
among fireflies.

GOD, WOMAN, EGG

After "Madonna," a lithograph by Edvard Munch

She never asked to lose innocence
like this: angels fingering her
the thrust of doves and roses at her door.
She had been soft and free.
Now the sky strikes her hair
lightning wielded by insomniacs
and her womb becomes the world's:
the feotus in one corner folded
skull and cross bones like a mouse
in a broom closet.

Each day its nails grow longer.
Sperm flow like the Jordan in her dreams.
She is God's purse, snapped tight.
She'll shrink as Jesus fattens
with her germ, elbows
the sac open and slides out, the spirit
a glue on his tiny thumbs.

RACCOON SKELETON AT LONG PLAIN CREEK

Wading upsteam we bump his carcass
with our ankles. He jiggles
like the needle of a compass
scattering silt until he's pure
milk white. When he steadies again
he sprouts a pelt of grime.
Tin shines through his skull.
Pickerel caress his collarbone.
He's soaking light
right through his sockets

letting the water run its tongue
in every crevice
of his frame. We link
fingers, looking down . . .
all the soft things are gone
bone gets its turn.

FIREFLIES

For Donald

I see them illumine
their gazebos in the elms
like the quaint electricity
of summer cabins
they flicker
cool, fire
I can finger without pain You

showed me, you
keep them in your pockets
in your eyes
knowing the bulbs they burn
in their bellies
are sweeter than the sun's
and true light travels
as they do, slow
and at random.

MERMAID

Waist up, I know.
The rest snakes away:
Scales fins side-slits.
My thighs inhale the ocean

My wrists and breasts sweat off.
This tail fools the pure fish
The sharks' sweet playmate.

But the manta-ray
The size of a big man's hand
All palm, does his deep dance
I join with just my eyes
The tiniest fish hugging him like jewels.

I'm a woman
simply combing her hair.

BUTTERFLIES ON AN ILLINOIS ROAD

the world is the color of pumpkins
the dirt along the road runs like cider
corn stands up straight in green fields when

      butterflies hundreds of butterflies

            the colors of lemons
and rust
            the colors of oranges
and emeralds
                striped
                      silver
                            gold
                                  black

      butterflies
            suddenly fly by
                      the windshield
banging their bare shoulders
on the car

BEFRIENDING THE WEATHER

All day long she dials
threatening weather
snow rain darkness
spins rainbows of shadow
calls clouds like cows
she ignores the eyes
of hurricanes aching for gusts
hard breathing trees
lakes stirred out of their cradles and winds
breaking the record
                      when she gets sun
stroke in her dreams she wears
a huge hat and heads north
until hoods and mittens
nibble the tundra like caribou
She is building an igloo
She will line it with ice
All day long dusk snow and night
are falling
She dials fire

INTIMATIONS AT THE LAKE, 1963

Skinny Salvador went in first, a diamond
flashing on his finger.
Then fat Ken Harris, his voice
already a man's. Holding

my breath I didn't
even feel the icy water
or the mud afraid
of brushing
their genitals mysterious
as fish in the dark
water the plump moon
floating near-by.

We slipped out, squirmed
with our backs
turned into our clothes
and walked singlefile
the way we had come.

GEORGE ABBE

MY FRIEND, THE DOCTOR

My naked foot was sheeted with blood,
a brilliant, glistening glaze.
But I felt nothing.
Nevertheless, anxious, I sent a little girl
for the doctor.

I saw him; he was a friend of mine.
He came leisurely down the street,
with a coterie of companions. They were dressed up,
costly, and clean. They took their time.

I stood with numb and mutilated foot. Casually
he examined it. But he could not tell me what
had done it, or what to do. I suddenly realized
I had walked a long way. It was odd.
I had no sense of pain.

The clean, bright faces of all the doctor's friends
bent toward me like a circle of flowers.
Powerless, I stood with the foot half lifted
and stiffening in its glaze of blood.
And the lovely-apparelled, well-to-do people watched.

A SKILL IN KILLING

Through the hanging turkey's mouth
I drove a needle in,
straight up into its brain.

I felt the tissue give;
the will to live
ran scarlet on my hand;
and the breathing beak
gaped at my work.

Revolted, I forced myself.
This was the neatest way,
science had said: strike
the needle deep,
up through the mouth's roof;
the nerves are paralyzed,
the feathers made loose.
But as I probed and drove,
the tissues of my brain
broke with a thought that moved,
a pin-prick gentle as love.
Yet, numb I could not feel.
Not method nor resolve
made the act real.

I SAW AN ARMY

I saw an army coming against the sun.
Its men were faceless and its banners dead.
No cheering voice was lifted—no, not one.
The broken flesh of wounds forgot to bleed.

Upon their shields they bore their children's limbs
Seared in the oven of atomic glare;
Their belts were fission; and their armor gleam
The dust of blasts beyond the stratosphere.

Pricked was their skin and threaded white with steel;
The flame of rockets writhed along their thighs;
A chemistry of missiles bent the knee
And clothed the sorrowing mouth, the darkened eye.

Yet in their ranks they marched upon the sun,
With hands hung weaponless, with cindered cheek,
And spectral footstep faint as desert wind
That fails before it finds the strength to speak.

From death, the burning core of light, I watched,
And cried with soundless throat, "Beware! Beware!"
But deaf they moved, straight to what I had sought:
The fire of mastery, the target of power.

LAST PATCH OF SNOW

I'm not sure why I touched it.
A crocus tip can be more dazzling,
and a boy would rather throw dice
or marbles than be soft-hearted.

But the snow was the last,
in a corner between tree and wall.
The far crow answered things I had never asked,
and the wind, nearly April, moved
the buds. I almost remembered what I'd felt
in the long blizzard; I nearly recalled
the power of my legs driving the skis.

Or was it the thought of a kitten, white,
who slept under earth I'd turned
myself in spring, a corner of the garden
withdrawn and secret, where, shaken,
the white wild cherry blossom fell?

I cannot tell. But I knelt
as I did when told, in older people's prayer,
and taking the snow upon my palm,
saw the warmth of sun turn it to water,
the shudder and tremble, a tingling light,
I heard the crow, crying toward the river land,
the corn to fall, the hot suns of tomorrow;
and sorrow older than my memory flowed
from the fierce cold into my palm's blood.

DICK ALLEN

STAYING MARRIED

People who remain flabergasting for a lifetime
breathe deeply and collect stories of heathens
and are almost always sexy
as a senator's wife —
her dress split up
to the thigh
and they have closets of masks
with godawful expressions;
and Robin Hood hats, and belts of raw leather
and white sport jackets and high collar dresses
and scars on their elbows; and books
of Chaucerian wisdom;
and they change without caution.
In the middle of a rush of life, they change;
they take off their clothes and howl at the moon
or draw you diagrams of three lost souls
or utterly become
cool and sane as a river
in a state of good crops and good weather —
these people
who are never quite done
with faces butterflies would have
if they were human
astonish me,
astonish me with their love,
red curtains and songs about eyes.

THE WRITER'S HOUSE

I am going to make up a legend.
It is going to concern a pink house in Connecticut.
There are going to be four people in my legend.
A husband, a wife, a son, and a daughter.
Their house is about to be surrounded by trees.
The lawn grows higher and higher.
Sometimes, the curtains are not opened for days on end.
Lights are seen at all hours of night.
The husband has long hair and a terrified look in his eyes.
The wife wears barely any clothes and she looks beaten.
The son is always reading books and other children don't
like him.

The daughter screams so loud it shakes the woods.
They haven't had a visitor for months.
You hardly ever hear the television playing.
You see the husband sometimes walk in the rain.
It is rumored they are not well off.
Where they came from, no one seems to know.
One neighbor has reported seeing candles burning.
Another heard some moaning late at night.
The phone is unlisted.
Stories grow around the house as grass gets higher.
It becomes "the house where strangers live."
Fact becomes legend.

DEPRESSION: MY FATHER SPEAKS TO MY MOTHER

How we lived through that
time of no promise,
when always between us were
radio voices
and hoboes marked our door
with yellow chalk X's,
neither of us knows.

Each week we checked out five
American novels
featuring a good
guy beating a bad,
from the adult shelves
of our public libraries
and brought them back to read.

Saturday nights, we spent
discussing fate with friends
who were rich.
They gave us cheese and sherry
along with advice
on how to be happy,
and their minds held our hands.

Driving home one night
we ran out of gas
and I walked two miles
on a road where highway crews
were almost unknown
while you waited, crying
because it was not strange to be alone.

Like the others, we knew
one horrible answer:
I would march up
the gangplank to Europe
while you might fold
Red Cross bandages, with hope
my blood was neither hot nor cold.

When I came back
your hair was dyed, your kiss
was five years old
but you wore a new dress
and I had been
promised a job. On such
a day even penguins can happen.

AN AMERICAN GOTHIC

There is a woman in a white or blue
negligee running
across a lawn at night.
Behind her is a huge dreary mansion
in which something is screaming.

The woman has one hand half-covering
her mouth. Her negligee is torn —
exposing a bare Victorian shoulder,
a flash of pink ankle.
Somewhere, a fire is beginning.

This is the highpoint: that run
across the wet grasses
toward the small town lying
asleep in the happy trust
of power, wealth, decision.

67

Horrow! Horror! How could
the beautiful spinster not know
that such evil lurked
on the staircase, and in
her handsome master's arms?

It must be a dream. The world
is basically filled with good
unintelligent people
who only wish to drink water
and dance in the fields.

Such people do not leave ghosts
to peer in the windows
with faces blood-drained, nor rattle
doorknobs, stand in a dim
room with fixed views.

It must be a dream. There is always
a logical reason
for apparitions, and old
muttering women
to deliver strange parcels.

And no one in the small
town cemetery has ever
opened her casket and dug
her way up through loam
to seek revenge, or a lover.

A dream. A dream. But how
real seems that hand
which touches your hanging wet hair —
the cat so suddenly hissing
at a breeze through the room.

Your telephone is tapped. Someone's breaking
into a safe, downstairs.
You receive crisp letters in
the afternoon mail:
secrets, secrets, a dream!

NORMAL LIVES

They are out-of-date
as porches
and women being coy about their breasts,
white washing machines:
unaltered lives
of catch-as-catch-can,
shadows trailing through the leaves;
and we miss them,
drive up to Maine
to look for Andrew Wyeth's house,
or someone so happy
the coast wind blows his hair crazy
as he talks about rain
and what it does to the ocean,
rocks and the sand:
normal lives,
indian heads,
lives seen backwards through a telescope,
beautiful, dangerous, watching,
eye into eye.

THE PRESENT

The present is such a lovely place
sparrows fly through it
and sunlight shines into it, day after day;
folk hymns are sung in it; out
in Nebraska two children
toss a softball back and forth;
sighing, a lovely young woman
lies back in the present with her thighs apart,
adoring her lover;
men lean from
open car windows; they watch
the present go by
their lives, other lives, and they think
of swimming in April.
Into the present
comes a quietness. The stars
begin to replenish;
it is a summer evening on the planet Earth,
fireflies jounce in the darkness,
crickets, treefrogs. You never
knew such contentment.
Strolling, thoughts to yourself,
you feel the present is a valley, a refuge,
a compromise
between past and future
and toss a stone at the river,
race your own wife to your door.

BRUCE HOLSAPPLE

VIII. 1969 — For Sherry

I send these wild roses
to you & thru the mail
they fade — the red petals &
yellow eyes become brown
& wrinkled, but they maintain
the delicate air about a rose —
the idea in which moments
rise like monuments to
bloom & decay — So take them
in your hand, as near to light
as the heart stands.

24/VIII. 1972

Quiet faces
of the moon
in a field of
Queen Ann's lace:
I've no response
but to bloom

UNTITLED

A short cut
under the spruce,
my right foot
finds a place
in the roots —
bark gone years
contact: a form
of friendship

71

UNTITLED

working
in a stupor
frustrated
I prayed

this came,
isolated

huge purple
vulva of iris,
Grotesque

& clumps of
yellow chickory

long-stemmed
topple in
the rain & break
the stalk

VII. 1972

I polish, cook, or clean my nest
silently forming these diamond-like things:
lightning flash, or when I've left
or lost enough of myself
the words loosen from my breast
an explosion of feathers:
my heart aches into the sky
like a bird which I
shoot & eat for you.

72

NAPOLEON ST. CYR

LEAVING THE FLAG OUT ALL NIGHT

A year ago, on what was probably
some crazy weekend I left the flag out,
Friday night, Saturday, day and night.
It's been out since.

Through rain, starlight, darkness,
bleached in the sun, for a reason unsure
of. A year now, and know it's me out there
hanging on a cheap pole, in darkness,
myself. Or

America and I, the two of us
so sewn together that we both should
hang limp in rain, or whiplashed in storms,
wars and massacres.

Cheap flag too. Thought that
as weekend flapped into week,
week into two, two into three,
month into months, sometimes draped
on a casket, sometimes
just hoping that the colors
would hold fast.

The colors have run;
the borders between courage, purity
and innocence blur with one another,
and justice turns a grayer color.

The stripe ends are in shreds,
and after all these rains
how the colors bleed.

73

ORIENTAL

The living room walks softly on Bukara,
tapestry size. Bukaras are not the best
but they do for the ignorant.
Bukara, a misnomer, a friend tells me.
For us, all there is, all that matters
are its colors, black, white, and red.
At the borders some fancy knot work —
intricate frame for a picture.
Surrounding and bordering that, black
spearheads march one upon the other, pivot
column left at corners and move on as a horde.
All around with these, strange shapes,
bursts of beating Aryan eagle wings rise
to fill the room which shakes
to black wings of war. Interspersed
white eagles deceive, but both with faulty
weaving, imperfect —
unfinished as though its maker
nomad rushed to tie a knot and fled
across the steppes of Turkestan.
And had he fled again from this center
design tracked in column of invading
elephant feet? Ghengis Khan has come to that
pattern, and to that far corner
where other black wings have lost a feather;
and is it Tamerlane who explains
a new dye — that patch of unmatching color?
The last foot of rug is crowded and unlike
the maker, done by the son? Inherited with the loom?

With the right large map this rug might cover
the whole weave and shuttle of brutal armies,
the suffering desert, from the Mongols
to the Black Sea, soaked in one
dominant color of old and ancient blood.

74

In memory of Hitler and our times
we've placed at our front door
a small one to match it,
now properly itemized in a will for our heirs.

FRIEND WITH SPINNING ROD

You stood in our small boat
casting out into air
as men with a net, arcing yours
one thread at a time,
a spider spinning out monofilament
criss-cross to cover the water —
reaching out beyond yourself
from where you were to where you were not.
Next to lotus blossoms
you dragged
the surface, and with other lure, the shallows.

And when that lost sea bird
(he seemed not to belong on our small lake)
coming from nowhere, curious,
glanced us in the eye,
banked as you cast your lure,
darted down to strike,
veered as sudden — a claw from his prey —
and soared parabolic merged on high,
I watched your face against the sky.

ARTERY OF THE SEA

Heraclitus dwelled
on tributaries of the sea.
Man could not step into the river Same twice:
same man in the not-the-same river;
twice makes
not-the-same man in not-the-same river.

Blood leaves the heart asking, out to the finger tips
of the world, and
returns to color the human heart.

What beats on a summer day,
between a day in summer and the breaking sea —
an imperative, which beckons us
to bathe
in the permanence of its motion.

ALL MEN ARE . . . SOCRATES IS . . .

I was no taller than a seedling then
when my parents told me so.
The parochial nuns said the same:
Their black shrouds made their
words sound so right.

The camp in Maine we've built since then
is smack in the prevailing wind
leeward
of an incredible hemlock
shallow rooted as we ran up there
bomb shelter.
We've pondered the thing and
watched it nod our way on windy days.
Lightning's torn its hide twice.
It's too big for any proposal of mine.

Some windy day, some sudden moment
when we are inside . . .

T. ALAN BROUGHTON

TO THE OTHER SIDE

The lake is sky
hung with trees.
I slip from my dock
on the shove
of a foot.

He also leaves
from the other side.
We do not dip
our paddles.
We drift.

He glides
from the mirror
I approach.
No leaf shakes.
The light is morning
and memory slides.

Our face converges
to the center.

THE PEOPLE CANNOT SPEAK

We walk tonight
in the valley of our bones.
Here no skin is stretched
on hollow wood,
no song except
the dry shake of our steps.
Grass is withered
and even mice
who could have tucked
through ankle and rib
are sketched in brittle parts.

We walk where the moon,
our only heart,
is steady in light,
where nothing beats between
the metatarsel and teeth.
This is the loom
for weaving cloth of wind.
We cannot read
the pattern of our shadows.

We sit down
on the spread wing of a pelvis.
Dry lightning tangles
once in the rootless tree.
If only we could name
each bone, each bone
would join
and all this valley
flow with sinew.

The sky shakes twice
Our tongues lie down like slate.

A GIFT FOR MARY MACLANE

Will the wise world itself give me in my outstretched hand a stone?
—Mary MacLane: Oct. 28, 1901

I hand you:

stars, nearer than ever
sewn on a warm shawl of night

the rock buttes
dipped in your dreams
to turn them green

a book
whose pages strip you
back to the small point
of your birth scream
and change it to laughter

a touchstone
                to open your womanly lips
                with the tongue of need

                to hold the breast gently
                a dove cupped for release

                to spread your thighs
                with the limber root.

Stretch out now
and take my gift.
Wherever you lie
I bring this marrow poem.

THE CAVE WHERE NIGHT SLEEPS

It is a cave of red stone.
Water finds a way out of its walls
and gathers in a pool.

The wood tick waits in the grass
at its edge. It seizes the deer
and grows fat.

The animals leave their prints,
as do men who have drawn
the wounded bull,
the maimed and supplicant hand.

You may stand at the far end
your back to the wall,
bent as a scooped out shell
of space, and the light of day
at the mouth will hurt.

You stand in the bow-bend of the horns
whose points are stars.
Behind you the black wind hangs
sleeping on the peg of day.

I have walked out of that cave,
my back stained and wet,
numbing already to its last cold rest.

PLANET DREAM

rising through sky
the center of blue
                turned
without falling
                breathing
the light
         no stars or moon
and arms outstretched
                  my legs
akimbo
       whirl on whirl
is this water or sky
shapes and folds me
                I am
full of blue
          naked
my skin wet
           my new
eyes
     hips and wheeling sockets
I am turning turning
                  trees
rocks and rivers rise
from my fire
          white arch
of bone
       fingers and tongue
rolled forever in blue
water and air
             plunging
layer on layer

SNOW CHANT

I.   white seed tossed on glass
sprouts darkness
                        night
lies on its fresh
bed
    white fire
held in the husk

II.   flakes of moon
                    ash
of her burning
                   I hold
my palm face open
she takes my heat
I am buried by
      her distant touch

III.   winter's lily
cold petals always
unfolding
                numbed
fragrance
                nightstemmed
drawing its sap from ice
flower of sleep
                 its last
dream was earth
before it grew down
from the sky

IV.   wither to steam
untie the grass
                and bind
yourself to the pool
the river snake
                follow
the cold sky
over the sea

83

DIANE KRUCHKOW

WHILE THE TV IS SHUT OFF

in the dead screen
I see you sleeping
in living color
& hear you snore
by my side

you are public now
they are all watching
the crazy man
who yells down
the crowd taken in
on this day of peace

the kerosene lamp glows
thru your dreams
light years beyond frustrations
to days when innocence said
there was something to be done
something beyond screaming
to the patrons at the local bar

tomorrow
will be sun or snow
or perhaps rain
at any rate
the birds know
which way to fly
& how to adapt
to the wind

84

POEM

for the 5th time
it came
the mosquitoes knew

it came over the towel
near the closed tent flaps
the lemon scent
of too much citronella
poured thru the pines

the mosquitoes noticed
energy reaching out
in filaments
for the 5th time it tried to grab
onto the tent
the campfire

candles burned
near the image of a girl
with hemlock in her hair
watching

THE CITY IS FALLING APART

the city is falling apart
there is a sense
that the pigeons are gone
& spittle hangs from the lips of businessmen
painted smiles on sides of streetcars
light clouds too dark for fireflies
only death walks with no mechanical key
toward the one in the corner crying
the hands of the clock keep moving
toward the one in the corner crying

85

POEM

she didn't know it yet
she knew
it was unfurling
like a marsh of
fiddlehead ferns
into a reaching . . .

a bass fell over the dam
onto a hook
in the distance
there was a noise

echoes of the intangible
slither
beyond the current growth
(snakes still scare)

on the other side of the dam
rumbles of traffic
fall into rainbows

POEM

"the camera records
the smile of a happy snake"
is that what i am the
other side of the apple there
is an eden somewhere in the stars
I see it in your beard
the snake has eaten a rabbit
it was not cheap

86

PUTTING THE CROUTONS BACK INTO THE JAR

shut off the radio
& play the record
shut out the possibility
of intrusion
the record you have heard before
the needle rests
safe within its grooves
pianos & violins
scream
familiar pain
the fireplace performs
you have no fear
of snow

SABINAS HIDALGO

dancing
to the sound of the night
all over back yard America
dancing
to the dungeon stone
& the gloom
tapping right foot on the ground
to awaken spirits
the spiked tooth coyote howls
rising from the underground
volcanoes trapped beneath skyscrapers
from mouth to mouth
tip to tip
old tumbledown holy America
tumbling down

FLOYD C. STUART

BALANCES

Hawk's sudden weight
on the limb would almost
fling him.
He swings

        hooked
feather-greaved.

            In the mind's eye
he lifts great slow wing
over field
        swift
           high
poised against the mind's sky

                    fragile balance

his hunched heft on the branch,
a man's flight out from it.

HARD EDGE OF BEAUTY

Deep in Deering Oaks,
bright among the ancient trees,
floats a solitary swan
like a delicate suspended note.
She contemplates the silence of her perfect self.

Mozart must have known how one sweep
of the graceful wing can shiver
a strong man's strongest bone.

SIX STATUES IN A PARK

They sit among music of waterfall leaves,
unhearing, six sobering monoliths, cold
this morning in the crucible of summer,
unmoved by wind-danced dapples like bold
hands of fugitive and hungry Eves.
They are six great men, unsexed, convened
to brood in this garden of deflowered virgins.

Burns, for one, stares past a cigarillo
stuck between his granite fingers, juice,
flesh, bone turned death-cold stone.
We scratch obscene grafitti on these bases
to rage against the void, to reassert our potency,
oblivious to the flickering leaf light
consuming our rebellious faces.

PILOT

The land has sunk to black
and towns begin to glitter.
A few lights track
like slugs with dim design.
But here the sky is limpid hues
of the wildest parrot of the mind,
and nothing even slowly moves.
All is locked in one high sound's core
except, when brushed by air,
the fragile metal creaks
like a woman stirring in a kitchen chair.

STONE AGE

(in the therapy room)

His great bald head, trembling weightiness
on the edge, almost rolls onto me.
Flourescent lights strike up mica glints.
The cheeks are sinkholes stubble starts to cover.
His knuckles in the nurse's hands gleam . . .
thin stream water cupping over stones.
His feather touch surprises: the handshake
once would heft like quartz. But a breeze still
sparkles the eyes; veins shine through temples
and forearms, unmined. If stone could speak.

MIRA FISH

CAPE COD MURDERS, 1968

Always, the damage is irreparable.

Here, the wind is right for suicide,
blowing up from Sagamore and down into Truro;
there, the dead girls lie pale by scandal.

The highway curls over Bourne Bridge, but a widow
has jumped this morning: the season demands endings
here and they come in fashion, dark as
the New York Buicks.

On the beach, beyond the imagination, an old
dispute continues until cliffs erode and
ugly cottages pile in with their wood bones afloat.

This is the trick: to watch the big road end at
the tip, or to dawdle alongside; there is one
house, its shutters nailed down and we name its
end, the eyelids of each summer,
embalmed.

POEM

You jam your arm into the white air
and would wait there
with seed in your hand until
suppertime.
You are patient with the chickadees,
winter birds,
hungry beyond your feel,
and your patience is a quick-draw

challenge to their hunger;
　　but you tease me
saying bird's legs are delicacies,
and I half believe you would catch one—
just to win.
　　And then some small bird
flits to your hand and away again
with one seed in its beak,
and suddenly you have won over
the jungle
the sea
and the air
all at once.
　　A triumph over one quick
skinny bird
hungry, probably, for only your
eyes.

POEM

Four miles out the tide curls in
like a beagle's ear
as we lunch together in the stiff suit of noon,
of north light in May.

Our postures belie us. We swallow the silence,
roughage dressed in vinegar;
we are the windfall, injured.

On the sill, a tomato fattens
like a magic frog; outside, a garden swells from
the sand, and all the tones urge
growth;

92

today we do not make dialogue,
but you abort the tomato, slice clean, skin
to core, and all comes bundling out
in jell:

seeds, belly, and plasm catch me tight and still,
the rising of me settled in my womb like stones.

"OH, SAY, MR. TOFFLER"

The heart of my day holds no
center: genitals come
undone and Midtown neon fades. Here,
the cellar door has lost its hinge and
rattles a hard rhyme to wind; and so what
vortex holds necessity?

Mother calls and the past
berates and the moon,
old maid, blooms wrong.

They've done it. All busy minds,
sharpened points, the typeface of
change explode to sense. The moon passes
backward and the mad tumble of roses comes
clean to August while my man beats
off down in
7A.

PREGNANCY

yours is a benison,
the supper bone
to dogs.

You have been starved
for a child;
a miracle, your womb;
a fairy tale.

But your conception is
wrong!
He will not be born a hero,
the Christ, Good News.

Will you learn this motherhood
is an artist's work?
that the child, his cry
at birth, is
haiku?

MICHAEL MCMAHON

THE DOSSIER

1. military officers from Prussia
   harrangue boarder guards
                      no one may leave
   some General has left a monocle
   and an epaulet dye drains from
   upon my good name

2. what if some night the walls open
   and two men from Duluth walk in
   with a girl I screwed in 6th grade
   and graphs of the times
                      I masturbated

   they say "we know of you"

3. soldiers herd my life's gestures
   into box cars with cattle prods
   at dawn
               they are deloused and smell
   like boys sweating in locker rooms

   the air is fat with burning flesh

4. the dossier is my mother speaking
   of nice girls
                  it holds my life like
   a doctor and demands I cough

   its tongue turns my blood to ink
   and whispers "we are coming soon"

WHY FIRES ARE LIT DECEMBER 21ST

once white people believed the blood
turned white in winter
                          when tree sap
thickened beneath bark gone glass in
sleet when they split birch chunks
to wake the fire that slept inside

their knuckles told them of a cold
curled and hibernating in the bones
akin to the cold that cracked skin

they carried this with them like bad
memories
              at night in bed it pawed
and sniffed at their hearts by day
it growled behind their eyes

                                some lit
fires to drive it deep in the flesh-
cave
        others slit wrists to let it out

A POEM FOR RICHARD SPECK

walking into a hall full of nurses
must be liking exploring cartons of eggs
in the supermarket dairy case

what would one do but suck the shells
dry or smash them to know the tingle
of the white slipping through fingers

what is in a nurse a womb papered pink
that a hand can roam around and break
dozens of future children like chairs

one thinks of the way a bear rips up
a hive of its snout pulling away
soaked with honey egg yolks blood

MAIDENHEAD

friend of the albatross
and teacher of the satyr
mothers are rumored
to have used them for lap·dogs

but who has hunted it knows
its guile many men have been
down wind of one
                         then poof!
into the forest of the hair

in that jungle insects sing
Ave Maria
             and the dead are
carried to elephant graveyards
no one recalls

stalking it you will think
of the sun behind thin clouds
of a naked girl beside a spring
drunk with her own reflection

and hear a moan as if an animal
has crawled into the bush to die
set out sugar bear traps
track its blood to former lairs

you will never see one alive

THE POLITICIAN

we save fish heads we don't know why
some go jet then hard
as ebony others flake
layers of skin thin as butterfly wings

most scrape our noses raw for weeks
until the fish eyes turn concave
and fish lips opaque
as plexiglass shatter at a touch

our cat swallowed the jawbone of a fish
it bled the cat's gut full
two children let two skulls
slit their throats and tongues

we watched you stitch the wrent cat's
gut and yank each bone
from each kid
like a rabbit from a hat

but none of this has anything to do
with fish heads we swept
under our rugs for your visit
they still stink we will not vote for you

A STRANGER IN YOUR TOWN

I am in the corner of your eye all day
you see through me
like the translucent window of a bar
people not like you are having a good time behind
and resent it

98

perhaps the way my jeans squeak recalls the boys
you wanted to touch in school
perhaps my nose is missing like the phantom
of the opera's vague as cloud
you do not know

if I peddle women waiting above our heads
in cockroach rooms
or the men who do not care about your life
sent me to stomp your genitals in
like garbage cans

you dream my body blue beneath the riot sticks
of your gigantic police
in your stone face I see
you know me only by the murderous stoplight
in your eye

THE BIRTH OF MY DRINKING PROBLEM

let us say my drinking problem hangs
from my neck
like an albatross or crucifix
and you are a guest on your way to a wedding

I put my drinking problem into your mouth
like the Host
the arc of the bride's breasts forgot
you will perhaps see the beast slouch

it has of course the cheeks your mother
would have kissed
the mouth she yearned to wet-nurse
and the face of whatever it is you wed

my drinking problem bawls into the tin cups
of our bodies
until flooded we sink to sleep
in unfathomable gin where gills grow again

my drinking problem the only body that can
bear our true reflection

UNTIL THE COWS COME HOME

how long have the cows been gone

they are not sent cards at Christmas
the hands of milkmaids gnarl
from disuse
cattle rustlers must run for Congress

why are the cows not at home

they were sent to battle the invisible
perhaps they leaped the moon to amaze
astronauts
                and are mired on Mars
where they low for help in a canal

what will cows look like when they come

their tongues will resemble the babes
of pietas and beg the milk of kindness
we will pull the night over our heads
like the pelt of a wolf
                        to drive them off
when will the cows come home

when the stock exchange turns bullish
over China
                when the pigeons gather
like evidence in the roost
and our lives cannot pass through our lives

100

TED ENSLIN

THE WHEAT DISTRICT

"My father planted those fields
of yours
            to wheat.
He said he'd plant
so long as a day's journey
by horse and wagon
would take him to and from a mill
where he could have it ground."
"The fields are grown up now.
Dense woods.
Popple and maple.
You can hardly see
where they were."
"Yes. Times have changed.
We don't know
what the land is worth.
We thought we did, once."

Extending the district
from a dooryard
on the dark side of the hill
into the sun
where the wheat lay,
along these roads
to a mill,
            and
back again
one day's journey
(at the last of it
two towns away—
a tight race)

or the flow of one man's blood,
how far it might go
within the skin
to nourish stem and branch—
from leaf to root—
and nourished in itself.

Walk part of the route,
an hour's worth,
eyes closed.
A track known in early spring
by where the ground rises—
the sense of district—
that closes one
                        in it.

And of this district,
a fragility—
from snow to dust—
a single day—
that journey.
So — all things meet.
A lawful distance
what one takes.
A day's going,
sunrise to set—
down from the wheat fields
dimly seen—
before night'
dimly seen again.

THE DISTRICT: BOTH SIDES OF CHANDLER RIVER

It can't be a pocket—
cul de sac—
in that sense isolated—
crossed and crossing
U.S. 1***
Primus
the early seaboard road
laid out to connect
the several states.
This remained,
still does, with some flavor,
tuned by wood smoke
and slow speech—
lobstermen and other fishers
living here—
measuring the times
by periods of tide
more importantly
than by change of attitude—
method to get at
primal measure,
whichever way the wind blows.
Not occuring as some
                    quaint trap,
downeast for summer tourists,
though they come.
                    More pity
that the force of life
remaining
            does not touch
in other places.
The thread of road
has continuity only
in this fracture.

The district cut off
willfully.
Won't go from the sea
in ships or winds
to that other
           what

ever
      that other.
Fragile township
where the Chandler River rises —
debouches quickly
to the sea.

D. W. DONZELLA

TO MY FATHER ON PEARL HARBOR DAY

(1971)

You tried so hard to make me believe in this day.
We practiced together to get it down right.
For you I hated Japan.
For you I learned to be vengeful.
Like you I even tried recalling where I was on that day
(and settled on having been with you).
Every seventh since I could first help
we remembered.
We stood on your swaying destroyer-deck memory,
two Navy men remembering;
I nodding 'yes' to everything you recalled.

But surely there is something wrong this year.
The Japanese officer in the movie I saw last week
had straight teeth;
he spoke better English than you;
he had more sympathy for American prisoners
than for the Emperor's orders.
And the narrator in the prologue said that we knew
about the attack hours before.

Father, what am I to think now, thirty years after?
You listen to a Sony radio;
I drive a Toyota to school;
and that madman Hirohito is touring the world
perfectly exonerated and wearing medals.

What am I to think father? What am I to remember?
I was never there.

WINTER

Scrunched down in the seats
of my frozen car,
I told you with smoking breath
how I wanted to piss on the windshield,
both relieving myself
and clearing visability
in one masterful stroke.

You laughed like a tunnel
echoing trains.
And there while the engine warmed
and your head bobbed
in and out of your coat,
we made some sense of winter.

Winter used to come to my poems
a fat middle-aged woman in a hearse
wearing black.
She kicked apart sentences,
took on dominant personalities,
defied my images,
and generally sat up with me
like an unwelcome pushy aunt.

See how I've changed,
how winter has become a young girl
freezing in my car.

All the way home tonight,
fumbling with the heater,
we will laugh at the footprints I left
on the hood of this car.

CONSTANCE CARRIER

ELEGY

Here where the elm trees were
is only empty air.

Where once they stood
how blunt the buildings are!

Where the trees were,
sky itself has fled
far overhead.

We have lost the leafy shield
between us and that space,
that lonely tract, revealed,
the light too straitly shed—

and lost as well the lace,
the filigree, that gave
the works of men a grace
not theirs by right.

The world is smaller and larger
with the tall trees gone.
Through sunlight yellow as pollen
we walk where the elms have fallen.

We walk in too much light.

INTIMATIONS OF IMMORTALITY, CUTTINGSVILLE, VERMONT, 1880

Their idiom, their dimension,
was life; they spoke in its terms.
What vigor their houses have!—
deep-based, tall-windowed, updrawn,
towered, they rise like trees
from thin soil spruced into lawn
and shell-rimmed flowerbed,
toward a more spacious air.

Convinced they would live forever,
the men who set them there
took death in like an orphan
to be petted and wept over:
gave it homes ornate as their own—
mausoleum and mansion
speaking their certainties:
there was death, but there were no dead.

        (Life-size, frock-coated, white-
        marble, he kneels before
        a classic temple, and holds
        at an angle of reverence,
        a marble hat to his heart.
        His eyes—the pupils are carved
        deeply—yearn at the scrolls
        of a six-foot iron gate
        opening into the temple
        to show the cella, the shrine:
        a square white-marble parlor
        furnished with mirrors, two
        small wooden rocking chairs,
        and the busts of a child, a girl
        and a woman, on pedestals.)

Where indeed is thy sting,
O Death domesticated?
Manse, mausoleum: they bring
these men into kinship with those
who painted Etruscan tombs
a cheerful gold and red,
the odious word translated
into colloquial prose.

THE TAKEN TOWN

Who cared enough for the town to take these pictures,
blueprint or sepia, with their fading dates—
eighteen-seventy, say, or eighteen-eighty?
did he guess that there was an enemy at the gates?

As he stood on the green (it is there today, but smaller,
with fewer trees) to record the new hotel,
he could hardly suspect that, so, he was recording
some of the vanguard of that army as well.

They had breached the gates unheralded, unnoticed,
not in disguise, not creeping like scout or spy
on this hardly-more-than-a-village, with its cobweb
of straggling streets called Chestnut or Church or High

that met a walling-out wall, intangible, surrounding
the Hill and its villas, grotesque with turret and bay—
and a walling-in wall, much older, marking the limits
of a town with no river, and only two trains a day.

The villas, the park, the churches, had cast-iron fences;
wooden pickets protected the humblest lawn . . .
Cast-iron across the front of the Hotel Webster
was a balcony that the drummers would lounge upon.

The drummers were city-bred men, the drummers were
    transients
from a far half-rumored country of steel and cement;
and most of them saw themselves not as Alexanders
but as envoys by some Alexander sent.

If they were village-born, they had fled the village
and its walls and fences. Now, with a Cremo cigar,
their sales complete, they relaxed and spoke of the market,
or met in a kind of free-masonry down in the bar.

But, wall-respectful, the town did not heed the drummers,
though it made its gossip of other flouters of walls—
the banker-embezzler, or the Porterfields' daughter
who married so oddly, or the man from Tuckahoe Falls . . .

The town had a library now, and a Civil War statue,
and most of the oldest houses had been torn down,
but the drummers there on the balcony in the evening
were looking out over an almost feudal town

with walls around it and walls and walls within;
walls around Water Street, walls around the Hill.
The drummers would help make a city of it, some day,
but the town itself was intact as a honeycomb still.

Yet soon those fences would fall, those walls would crumble,
and the pattern would never be quite so precise again.
The trumpets were there, and the lamp, and the broken pitcher.
The drummers were Joshua's men, or Gideon's men.

NEAR THE OLD SLAVE FORT

Keta, Ghana

An old woman, naked,
clasping a garland of red flowers
to her shrivelled breasts
has waded, singing, into the Gulf of Guinea
She raises her arms and casts the flowers
into the waves

Beside the wall of Fort Prinzenstein Prison
the old man in his castle
of torn books, newspapers and old
cardboard cartons
has not raised his eyes

And I, who know nothing of their lives
pretend that I can find them in a poem.

THE LOST DEER

We found the deer
my father shot
beside the road
two seasons later
one hoof, the leg from
the shank down, a pile of hair. . .
that was all that was left.

We put the leg in a tree
to fool the others
coming half loaded from fishing
or visiting whores in Indian Lake:
"Jesus, a deer in the goddam tree!"

It was a weak joke.
We remembered the day we lost it,
a grey streak and a snapped shot.

Good hunters, my father might say,
if he were a poet, don't just work for death.
(Algonquin people hunted here: skin, meat, horns
and bones were food, clothing and ritual. They
drew circles to show where they lived with
deer, fish, birds and earth.)
We left a circle unclosed.

The woods had taken it back.
Coyote and raven, shrew and whitefoot
nibbled the bones like sugar cubes.
Even the soil was more fertile
where it fell.

But each of us said silent words
before we turned away.

FOR MY GRANDFATHER IN GREENFIELD CENTER

The water clock of melting snow
runs faster now,
the letters you write
with cramped and mis-spelled words
have overflowed my drawers, my arms
and all the rooms of this house
we share with the sun

In the old house
you turn the television off
Matt Dillion's face collapses
into a pearl.
Hearing wheels increase
with the season's flow
your eyes look for
the pale shoots of crocus
And less than a hundred sunsets
lie between us

Keta, Ghana

LEAVING THE PRISON

For my writing class in Comstock

Distance comes between us like a knife,
first only the edge, then twisted
to the width of the blade
with the click of each steel door.

Corridors smell of plastic,
pastel funguses root into concrete,
somewhere someone is pounding with a hammer
somewhere someone is always pounding
with a hammer.

At times the building shakes
as if wishing to launch itself at the moon,
but when night comes, it sinks,
a battleship between the mountains
and the men lie, ballast in its belly.

Only the guards seem free to float up to the sky
but some weight they cannot name holds them

they walk like divers with leaded shoes
calling old names beneath their breath
as they drift endless midnight halls.

HOW I CANCELLED MY LIFE INSURANCE

"FOR YOU. . .If you live to retire. . ."
The papers lie self-effacing as a shroud
on my desk. Only twenty-three
but already so close to triple indemnity.
The years fall like raindrops,
I'm soaked with human fraility.
"FATAL ACCIDENTS ARE INDISCRIMINATE!"
It goes on to say, discrete
as the best mortician.
"THEY TAKE THEIR TOLL FROM OLD AND YOUNG!"
I'm through before I've half begun.

It is summer,
the time when days are long,
the cicadas are filling
the elms outside with breathless song.
But now that the possibility of
DEATH to the COMMON CARRIER (me?)
has become so imminent —
the policy rattles like a snake,
a paper chain foreboding doom —
Do I have the strength or courage left
to even try to cross the room?

I leave the policy, folded now,
held down by a hundred of e.e.'s poems,
walk out of the house,
the song sparrow that nests
in the blue spruce
flies up and explodes into song.
Beneficiary of the sky,
leaves blow soft in the wind,
the days are long.

ROBERT SIEGEL

POET

Found out in left hayfield
under a crooked moon
bought in a green bottle
in a back alley in Wales
plucked from a rock
where the sea goes rabid —
at night the pink feet
wizen to little hooves.

The transparent extra lid
the elastic web hidden
between silken fingers
in a red wool mitten
or the nibbed horn buried
in a field wild with curls —
may be trimmed at six
burned away like a wart.

Though his violet irises
be put under glass
in a symmetrical frame
arranged for at school —
dangerous in adolescence
liable under the moon
to be changed to an elm
married to tulips.

Holds the earth like a marble
between finger and thumb
breathes through grasses

116

belches clouds
sprouts words like pimples
hoards his shame
evokes a sly lip
from a name.

Grown glues his feet
under the stars
holds his mind inside out
like a Klein jar
up to the world maybe —
maybe not —
his clothes hung about him
like an afterthought.

NUDE

Content in her skin she does not challenge
the blue shadow cast over most of her body,
waiting in the shade like a center of gravity,
so full, even the trees have travelled too far.

Her breasts steal the wind with surprise,
promise long savannahs of discovery
beyond the trembling compass of a flower
or tuft of weeds agog with her sweet breath

I stand in this museum looking,
blood sagging to my fingers and toes.
The sun is coming at me through the wall.
Clothes could never touch her, this one, put
beyond the night whisper and morning's flat red mouth
into the first turning of the light.

MAD DOG

That night the dog let night in
Moonlight bubbled down his chin

Spilling across the porch. Thoughtful, he
Tore the black grass, sniffed what he'd torn,

Bayed a silk slip weeping from a line.
We could not get to him in time.

Nor out ot it — two pearls, his eyes,
Crabbed sideways in the tide.

Purring, a car crouched two houses down,
Its blue eyes sifting, sifting through the trees.

Shapes sidled up, a low voice hung
Its noose about his head. Snarling, he
Kinked into the street. A shot —

He took the moon at a lope. We heard
His bark drift back like distant stars
A thousand years beyond their fires.

EGO

has thrust his nose under every board,
smelt out every wild carrot and white grub,
stucco'd the dirt with his tracks from side
to side, rubbed smooth the corner
posts, left his pink, red-bristled hide
on every barb of five strands of wire;

chewed the bark from the one scrub pine
that pitches a ghost of shade at noon,
bangs incessantly the metal trough-lid
at off-hours, chuffs down the white meal
raising a cloud around his ears, and cleans
each cob with the nicety of a Pharisee

tooth for tooth, squeezing contentedly
his small bagpipe voice as he mashes
corn with a slobbery leer and leaves
turds like cannonballs across a battlefield.
Meanwhile his little pink eye is
periscoped on the main chance —

the gate ajar, the slipped board,
the stray ducky that flusters through the wire —
saliva hanging from his mouth like a crown jewel.
His jowels shake with mirth under the smile
that made a killing on the market, won the fifth caucus,
took the city against all odds

No wonder we shake at the thought of his getting out
of his square patch, electrify the wire,
(At night we hear him thump his dreams
on the corrugated tin hut and shudder,
the single naked bulb in there burning
through our sleep like his eye!

take special dietary precautions against
his perpetual rut, except that March day
we drag the yearling sow to him
through mud up to his hocks. From that handseling
comes the fat litter — the white one for the Fair,
the spotted black to be slaughtered in November.

We don't show him to the neighbors, though in June,
framed by clover and bees stringing out the sun, he is
quite grand, an enormous blimp supporting
intelligent waggish ears, regally lidded eyes and
a pink glistening snout
ready to shove up the privates of the world.